Gifts Galore!

Fun Ideas To Support Ill Friends

By Jane Sterett

Illustrations by Chuck McDougall

PRESS

Gifts Galore!
Fun Ideas to Support Ill Friends
by Jane Sterett

Printed in the United States of America

ISBN 9781612153919

Unless otherwise indicated, Bible quotations are taken from The NIV Study Bible, New International Version. Copyright © 1985 by Zondervan Bible Publisher.

www.xulonpress.com

Table of Contents

Dedication

To all hurting, ill people who may be in need of a kind deed and loving action. I dedicate this book to you in hopes you feel a tiny bit better after receiving one of these gifts.

Introduction

"Do to others as you would have them do to you."

Luke 6:31

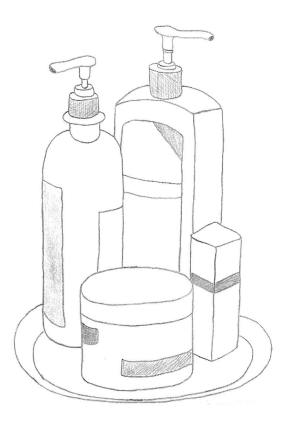

"What can I do to help?" Many people ask this question of themselves when a friend or relative is diagnosed with cancer, a long-term illness, or is about to have surgery. We all want to help and show we care, but we are not sure what to do.

This book will provide you with a wide array of gift ideas when your friends or relatives are faced with various illnesses. The goal is to eliminate your helplessness and empower you with many ways to provide encouragement to those who are ill or laid up. There are gift ideas for different situations, such as a hospital stay or a recovery at home, but you be the judge and choose which present is appropriate for your sick friend.

Being a supportive friend is the kind of person we all aim to be. No one wants to ignore those who are hurting simply because they are feeling insecure about what to do for them. Any gift will illustrate to the sick person that you care about them and are thinking of them. You are not one of those people who disappears from your friend during her rough times. You empathize with them in their troubles and illnesses, and are exhibiting both your love and God's love to them.

My prayer for this book is that you will gain fresh ideas, find a fun or meaningful gift, and deliver or send it to an ill person. Taking time from your busy life to do something for a sick friend has an impact on her. She knows she was thought about and loved by a good friend. You are giving her a boost and possibly a little happiness as she copes with her illness.

General Gifts

'A gift opens the way for the giver and ushers him into

the presence of the great.'

Proverbs 18:16

T hese ideas will work for most any ill person, but many are best suited for a woman. Most are simple and inexpensive. They convey the main message: the recipient is loved and remembered! Never underestimate how your kindness may touch the heart of a suffering person.

1. Purchase a personalized soft teddy bear for your ill friend. Shop at www.huggableteddybears.com. The front of the bear's shirt can be personalized in a number of ways such as "we miss seeing you at work" or purchased to fit a theme such as a baby shower, birthday party, or any special occasion. There are a

multitude of bears and shirts to choose from: nurses, doctors, colleges, and even a bear with a broken leg. Another fun option is to give the bear a name band to wear on his wrist. They come with any words you want on them, such as "Get Well Soon" or "Love from the Campbells." You may also reach them by phone at 1-800-829-BEAR.

2. Deliver small, decorated cookies, often made by someone who has a cottage business in their home. For example, a woman named Lisa in Palm Desert, CA, makes original cookies in most any shape you desire, all beautifully decorated. She can make band-aids, crosses, toys, flowers, and many more. Let her know what you are interested in, and if she is able, she will work with you on the shape and decoration. All the cookies come individually wrapped in clear plastic bags and tied with a ribbon. Shipping is available. Enter Lisa's website at www.Ohhlalabakingco.com. You can view samples of the cookies, but not purchase them

online. She would like you to call her so she can discuss with you exactly what you desire. Her phone number is listed on the website.

3. Make up a small basket of dried soups, hot chocolates, ciders, cookies and crackers. Michael's craft store generally has an assortment of baskets.

4. Buy a pretty mug and fill it with tea bags or accompany it with a bag of the patient's favorite kind of coffee.

5. Bake homemade cookies using one of your own favorite recipes.

6. Purchase wind chimes. There are a wide variety of wind chimes at www.Windchimes.com. The online catalog at www.redenvelope.com has a fun set of animal wind bells.

7. Purchase a gift certificate to one of her favorite restaurants. This might be a future treat when she is having a good day and would enjoy lunch or dinner out.

8. Ask any group of children, such as a Sunday school or preschool class, to draw or paint a picture for your

friend. Explain how the ill person will enjoy their art work. They might each try to draw the person lying in bed, colorful flowers in a vase, or some of their family members. They could draw the ill person alongside themselves. If they can write, have them write something on the picture and include their name. Most everyone enjoys children's artwork. Mail the drawings to the afflicted person's home. Besides boosting your friend by getting a packet of pictures, the children are getting a lesson in giving.

9. Buy a gift certificate for a manicure or pedicure at a local spa. If she has a regular nail salon, purchase it from there. Offer to drive her to the appointment.

10. Surprise your ill friend with a gift card to a local massage therapist. Ask other friends for a favorite recommendation if you are not sure who is a top therapist in town. A few therapists are well-known among the medical community, which might be a place to start. Be prepared for a variety of names!

11. Gather a few friends at a "paint your own pottery" shop. Each person could paint a mug, a plate or something fun for the patient. Add an encouraging word if there is space. If you want a group project, buy a large platter and have each person decorate a small space on the platter. The shop will fire the pottery for you within a few days. Google "paint your own pottery" to find a shop close to you.

12. Leave flowers or a small plant at her front door or gate for her to discover, along with a simple note. Finding a present at your front door is always fun.

13. Give some lovely note cards with a few stamps and a pen. She will always have thank you notes to write.

14. Send a card and note directly to the suffering person, letting her know you pray for her daily. Find out from her or a caregiver what exactly her prayer needs are at that time. It may surprise you!

15. Have one of the patient's grandchildren paint a picture for Grandma or Grandpa. Mount the picture and frame the artwork. Inexpensive frames are widely available.

16. Frame a new photo of the patient's children or grandchildren.

17. Ask a few friends over to your home. Make encouraging, loving signs for the suffering person on heavy tag board. Cut them into fun shapes and staple-gun onto sticks. Go to her home when she is gone or napping and pound the signs into the lawn so she can see them from a window. On Valentine's Day my sister and her friends made large hearts and loving signs for a very ill friend who was in Hospice care in her own home. Both the woman and her husband were especially touched and surprised when they looked out their window.

    Buy packages of wooden, pointed sticks at Home Depot, and heavy colored tag board at most drugstores. A friend and I copied this idea and made Valentine shaped signs for three different friends who were struggling with various illnesses. We put the patient's name and loving words on the hearts with cutout letters. Letters are easy to find at Michaels or any craft store. The signs were fun for us to make and a surprise for our hurting friends.

18. Pre-pay for a commercial cleaning service to come to the home at the ill person's convenience. If you are a very close friend or relative, you might even clean the house for her.

19. Look for small gift books. This type of book is found in most book stores, online, and in Hallmark stores. There are many small books about friendship, encourage-ment, or love and can be either humorous or serious. There are also small books with encouraging Scriptures at most Christian book stores.

20. Buy an angel made by Willowtree. There are a wide variety of white, resin 6-12 inch angels for all occa-sions. Look for angels of healing, friendship, comfort, love, joy, courage, spirit, or hope. Search the website at

www.Willowtree.info., or visit your local Hallmark store or Christian book store to view the angels.

21. Use paint pens to decorate a ceramic pot. The pot can be white or light colored. Use your creativity, perhaps personalizing it with her name, drawing flowers, faces, or words of love. An indoor plant in the pot is always appreciated.

22. Iron clothes for the family. This is a great help and very much an act of love. During a particularly hard time, my friend Debbie came from out-of-town to stay with me and ironed many piles of laundry! Another option is to pick-up the sick person's family clothes and iron them in your own home.

23. Buy a pretty box and fill it with positive sayings or Scriptures relating to healing, love, or friendship. Look up the Scriptures and print them on index cards. Suggest she read one everyday before she gets out of bed. Office supply stores carry many different sizes of boxes.

24. Write a funny but heartfelt poem especially for her.

25. Write a prayer for your troubled friend or for her family on a card, either handwritten or on the computer. One software source for making cards is www.Hallmark. com.

26. Print some plain postcards with encouraging words or a cute drawing on the front. Use your creativity! As an example, on the front print a saying such as "ROAD TO RECOVERY" and draw a road on the card. Make sure to print the ill person's address on the front also. Take the cards to an office supply store such as Staples or Office Max and have them printed for you. Put a post-card stamp on each card, and hand them out to friends of the patient. Have them write a note for the sick friend on the blank side at their convenience and drop the card in the mail. This is especially good for groups or organizations to which the patient belongs. Deliver the cards to the meeting so the postcards can be handed

out to a larger group all at one time. Stamped cards will

probably have a greater chance of being sent.

Hospital /Confinement/ Rehabilitation Gifts

"Dear Children, let us not love with words or tongue but with actions and in truth."

1 John 3:18

A hospital or rehabilitation center stay is never fun for the patient, so your goal is to lighten her day, if even for a brief moment. You want to illustrate to her that you care. These gifts are for the afflicted person who has to spend time recovering, and may or may not be in the hospital. A friend in the hospital may be too sick to receive visitors. If she is in a rehabilitation center, or confined to home and having to miss her regular activities, she may be feeling isolated and forgotten. These feelings can be lessened by knowing that her friends are thinking about her while she is recovering. If she desires company, pay a visit to her and bring a small gift.

The following ideas are useful for almost any situation where the patient has to be confined and is not able to get out and around.

27. Purchase a lap tray with fabric on the bottom, usually stuffed with small foam balls. This is comfortable against the patient's thighs, and provides a flat surface on which to write, read books, or draw. These are available through a website called www.Instand.com. From the homepage, click on "Assorted Bean Bag tables". In addition, I have seen lap trays at Borders. These trays are also handy for anyone to use as a television tray.

28. Shop for a decorated box to hold all the cards she is receiving. There are pretty boxes at Michaels craft store and Tuesday Morning, holding cards up to 6x9 inches. These boxes are often decorated, while the boxes at office stores are generally plain.

29. Buy a hummingbird feeder if your hurting friend is at home. The website www.RedEnvelope.com has a few

pretty ones. Click on the search box and enter glass hummingbird feeder. I have also seen them at Lowe's Home improvement Store.

30. Collect photographs from friends of themselves with the suffering person, recent or from years past. Put the photos into a small, beautiful album that is easily held while lying down.

31. Make a placemat of a group of pictures. Examples are flowers, gorgeous scenery, friends or family. Purchase tag board and have the office supply store cut it to placemat size, then make a collage with the pictures. When you are finished with the collage, laminate the placemat. Most office supply stores have a laminating machine. If you want it done quickly, bring the photos and a glue stick with you to the store and have an employee cut the board to the size of a placemat. Glue the photos on while you are at the store, laminate, cut the laminating paper with a 1/4" border, and BINGO, you have a gift ready to take to the patient immediately!

32. Take a picture of your friend's animal, enlarge the picture and put it in a frame. Many people miss their pets while away from home, and would enjoy looking at them while they lie in bed.

33. Look on the website www.allposters.com if you think the distressed would enjoy something new for their wall. The site has a vast selection of posters, including animals, flowers, beautiful scenery and much more.

34. Purchase a new stuffed animal that looks like her own adorable pet.

35. Search the Bible for Scripture verses regarding love and healing. Make a small scrapbook of the sayings or enclose them in a small photo album. Write a favorite verse on a large, decorated card for a bulletin board.

36. Find out whether your friend likes to wear pajamas or nightgowns. Go to any department store and purchase the softest nightwear for sale.

37. Shop department stores or specialty shops for comfortable, cozy lounging pants.

38. Purchase a soft bed jacket. These are available online at www.Amerimark.com. From the homepage, click on Anthony Richard's apparel, next click sleepwear. The bed jackets are pictured under sleepwear.

39. Deliver an assortment of magazines that your friend might enjoy. Keep them lightweight if she must remain lying down, as heavy ones may be hard for her to hold up.

40. Cut out funny cartoons from the comics that may be appropriate for her situation, and put them in a small notebook or scrapbook. Some of the daily newspaper cartoons have websites that contain old strips.

41. Offer to create a carepage for the patient on www. Carepages.com. This will keep friends and acquaintances up to date on the condition of the sick person. It is very simple to start a page, and you can update it at anytime with current information. The content is best written by someone very close to the afflicted and in constant contact with the caregivers. Include the

email addresses of the patient's friends and relatives so every time you update the page they will receive the new version as an email. The friends can then send notes back to the patient. If she is not able to retrieve the messages, print them out and bring them to the hospital for her to read. This is helpful to both the caregivers and the friends, as it eliminates endless phone calls and many repetitive emails. The person updating the page can go into as much detail as needed about the current medical condition of the patient. The patient can read and re-read the messages to them. It is uplifting to the patient to hear encouragement from friends.

42. Buy CD's of light music such as piano, harp, or singers you know she enjoys. Check beforehand if she owns a small, portable CD player that can be used while in the rehabilitation setting.

43. Massage your companion's feet while she lies in bed. (if she is not ticklish!) Caroline commented that this was her favorite gift while in the hospital.

44. Bring a gift bag filled with small bags of mints, pretzels, energy bars, small stuffed animals, or chap sticks. The ideas are endless!

45. Purchase fragrant hand and body lotion. Choose a light scent. Suggest a hand massage while you apply the lotion.

46. Bring her favorite coffee or tea drink from Starbucks or another coffee store. Check with the patient ahead of time to find out if a warm drink sounds appealing.

47. Talk with 7 friends and assign each person one day of the week to send a get well or encouragement card to the rehabilitation center. Hospital visits may be too short for this project, but each case is different. If the stay is less than a week, mailing the cards to her home address is the best idea. You may continue on after the person returns home. This is a guaranteed

way to make sure the afflicted one is receiving mail everyday.

48. Offer to orally read a book, poems, or Bible stories to a patient too ill to feel like reading. Keep it simple, short, and easy to follow.

49. Check out a captivating book on a CD from the library. Most libraries have CD's of books available for checking out a week or two at a time. Most can be renewed.

50. Rent an entertaining movie. Libraries often have movies to check out. Ask the hospital or rehabilitation center if there are DVD players or video players available to use in the room. Some patients may have their own. Find out what types of movies she enjoys, or if she has a favorite to watch again.

51. Deliver a book of easy crossword puzzles or Sudoko games along with a pretty pencil and eraser.

52. Take any fun retail catalogs you have received in the mail through which the patient might want to browse.

53. Deliver a journal and a pretty pen, if your friend is well enough to sit up and write. You might include a simple book about journaling.

54. Obtain a copy of the sermon given at her church the past Sunday. Some churches put a video of their sermons on their local church website. If the patient has a laptop, help them access the website of their church. Check with the hospital about wireless internet access in the patient's room or elsewhere in the hospital.

55. Purchase a ceramic mug with photos of friends, family, or pets of the patient. Kiosks that make them are sometimes found in shopping malls. Be sure to bring the pictures with you. Mugs may also be ordered online through www.shutterfly.com, wwwSnapfish.com, or www.Kodakeasyshare.com.

56. Buy a soft afghan or throw blanket. A warm blanket is comforting in a sterile hospital or recovery center. Some churches or cancer organizations have groups who make afghans to either sell or donate to patients.

Church groups often pray for healing over each afghan. Check on www.ebay.com for an assortment of afghans.

The Gift of knowledge

"Each of us should please his neighbor for his good, to build him up."

Romans 15:2

U nderstanding your friend's illness is a wonderful gift you can give them. Take time to research the internet and learn about their disease or surgery. For example, if you know someone recently diagnosed with Lou Gehrig's disease, learn what you can about the disease. The same goes for any difficulty or type of surgery your companion is going through. Although people will say "a little knowledge can be dangerous", it does help you to know some basics, whether a surgical procedure or a disease. Most ailing friends will be appreciative of your efforts. If researching the internet is not easy for you, and the patient is doing well, consider asking her to explain her disease. Let her know that you are genuinely interested in finding out about her condition. If she is married or has close relatives, consider asking them if they could help you. Let them know you want to understand more about the disease so you can be of comfort to your friend. Each person and family is different, but I have found that most distressed people appreciate a friend who understands the side effects and complications of their disease. If she is not interested in talking about her illness, she may still be grateful for your prayers.

Most people are touched by cancer, either through a friend, a relative, or personal experience. Learning some of the basics of various cancer treatments gives one a little more understanding of what the patient is dealing with. The more you can learn and understand about their cancer, the greater gift you are giving them.

Here are a few very basic facts about cancers. As a long term breast cancer patient, I am more knowledgeable about this type of cancer than any other type.

All cancer tumors have unique characteristics. Two friends diagnosed with breast cancer at the same time might each receive a different medication, because the treatments are not all the same. Each person's tumor is individually evaluated and the treatment is based on findings from the lab. It simply happened that their cancers were found in the same body part. This is confusing to people and hard to comprehend, but is true. Some cancers are slow-growing and non-aggressive, while others are fast to grow and spread. There are a multitude of different chemotherapy drugs. If your friend says she is getting "chemo", that doesn't necessarily mean the same "chemo" as another cancer patient. It is similar to taking cold medicine for a cough; not all cough medicines have the same ingredients in them. Some of the drugs come in pill form that the patient takes at home, while others need to be given by an infusion, meaning a liquid drug is given through the veins. Patients sit in a recliner and read or sleep while they are waiting for the liquid drug to finish. Often they will be in the recliner between 1-3 hours.

Chemotherapy doesn't always mean hair loss. If hair loss is one of the side effects, however, it will take around 3 weeks for it to begin to fall out. When treatment ends, it will most likely be a month before any hair begins to grow again.

The side effects of chemotherapy are varied. There is no predicting how one will feel afterwards, but often a person will have some days of feeling tired, their body may ache, or they might feel nauseated. Some people will be confined to their homes, while others will live a fairly normal life. Often the intravenous chemotherapies are given a few weeks apart, allowing time for recovery before receiving it again. There are more chemotherapy drugs available all the time, and they can have a wide range of side effects. Most people will suffer from one side effect or another during their initial treatments.

The chemotherapy drugs that come in a pill form are sometimes not as harsh on the body as the intravenous, or I.V. drugs. Yet again, it depends on the make-up of the tumors, the aggressiveness of the cancer and how the side effects impact the patient. The same drug given to two people may produce different side effects in each person.

A newer class of drugs for treating cancer is called Monoclonal Antibodies. I have been fortunate in receiving one of these drugs for over 9 years. These are drugs designed to target very specific cells on the person's tumor, and are given intravenously. They are currently being used in all kinds of cancer, but only if the patient's defective tumor cells match up specifically with the drug. These drugs mimic antibodies the body naturally produces in the immune system. The patient generally does not have the harsh side effects as they sometimes do with chemotherapy. But as I have said before, everyone responds differently.

Another method of attempting to rid the body of cancer is radiation therapy. This is accomplished by targeting the cancer with radiation beams. Radiation is sometimes given after surgery to catch and destroy any remaining cancer cells that may have been missed. It can also be the primary treatment for the cancer. The side effects from radiation therapy often depend on what part of the body has been radiated. As an example, ovarian cancer patients tend to have digestive issues following radiation. Fatigue is generally a common side effect to any radiation.

Metastatic, or advanced Stage IV cancer, is a cancer that has metastasized, or spread, from one body part to another. If you have breast cancer and it spreads to the liver, you do not now have liver cancer and breast cancer. You have breast cancer that has spread to the liver. If you get a tumor in your brain, you do not have brain cancer. It is breast cancer that has moved to the brain. I personally have found this to be a very common misperception about advanced or metastatic cancer. Typically, metastatic cancer of any type is not curable and the person will most likely be on some kind of drug for the rest of their life. The goal of most treatments for metastatic cancer is to prolong the life of the patient, hopefully for many years.

Gifts for Cancer Patients

"Be devoted to one another in brotherly love. Honor one another above your self."

Romans 12:10

T here are ideas in this section for an assortment of gifts. Look for one that might be a match for your friend and how she is coping and what she is feeling at the moment. I have divided the gifts into two categories: chemotherapy and radiation treatment. Many ideas are interchangeable between the two categories or can be used for other illnesses. The point remains that you are letting your friend know you are remembering her with love, and you care about her.

Gifts during Chemotherapy

54. Caroline knew she was facing surgery and chemotherapy for ovarian cancer. She helped herself feel a
little more in control by gathering her good friends at
a tea house before the surgery. She had already been
through breast cancer treatments and knew that she
likely would have times of not feeling well during her
recovery and treatment. She had a list of tasks that she
needed covered while she was recuperating. Knowing
her friends would want to help, she had each friend
choose an area where she was comfortable. One job I
enjoyed was to research the internet for the latest information about ovarian cancer and new drugs, clinical

trials, or related topics. Examples of other assignments chosen: cleaning her house, bringing a couple of meals to her husband, planting spring flowers in the yard, and driving her grandchildren to practices. Everyone felt so positive about helping. Any group of friends could gather, brainstorm, and come up with a plan tailored to the needs of the patient. Caroline gave all of us a gift that day!

Remember, these ideas may be used for any person who is not feeling well.

55. Drive your friend to the doctor. Offer to take notes or tape record the appointment while the doctor speaks to the patient. For an important appointment or when something about the routine treatment is changing, having someone in the room taking notes enables the unwell person to concentrate on what the doctor is saying. The notes help the patient to remember all the doctor's information and instructions.

56. Gather a few cards from the patient's friends before the first chemotherapy appointment. Put them in a fun basket or bag, and surprise her during her appointment while she is sitting in the recliner. The first treatment is somewhat nerve-wracking as the afflicted person may be feeling overwhelmed. Having cards to read might take her mind off of her surroundings for a few minutes.

57. Give a novel that you have read and know is a fast-moving, entertaining story.

58. Bring a basket of food items to her home. Before you give this, make sure your friend is not suffering from nausea. A person with nausea from chemotherapy treatment will often be particular about what her stomach can tolerate. Ask ahead of time what kinds of food sound more appetizing. Cold food sounds good to some, while others may only want soups or breads.

59. Research wig shops if your friend will be losing her hair. Ask other friends who have lost their hair for a recommendation on the best shops. Give the cancer

patient the name before she loses her hair. Choose a shop that makes appointments and spends time with the patient. During my many years with cancer, I have received more phone calls about wigs than any other cancer issue. Many times it is a friend of the person about to lose her hair. It is reassuring to know that the patient is able to have a wig that looks very similar to her real hair.

60. Accompany your friend and help choose a wig. Second opinions are often appreciated. It is helpful to accomplish all this before she loses her hair, as then she will have her wig ready and waiting when her hair falls out. Turn a sad day into a fun one by celebrating the new wig over ice cream or lunch. Some women say that losing their hair was the worst part of the cancer experience. Others are just glad to be getting rid of the cancer. Everyone reacts differently!

61. Access the American Cancer Society website for items to buy for the person with cancer. The address of the

site is www.acsgiftshop.com. Once you have accessed the site, shop by category to view the various products.

62. Look at baskets containing specific cancer products that can be purchased through www.Chemobuddyclub. com. There are many gifts relating to breast cancer, as well as some that could be for any cancer. Once you access the site, click on the tabs to bring up the gift baskets, breast cancer gifts, and individual gifts.

63. Host a video party in your friend's honor. Invite a gathering of her friends and relatives to your home, emphasizing to them that the party is to be a surprise and the patient will not be there nor know about it. Have her friends come to the party prepared with something short to say, read, or perform on camera. Explain that whatever they choose to do is up to them. Short poems, songs, or the whole group singing together is fun. A group of old friends from our former out-of-state home town had a party where they sang songs with a ukulele for accompaniment, recited poems, or

simply talked to the camera. The singing was all done with a lot of laughter and fun, while the individual stories or poems were touching. The hosts of the party had a relative put together the DVD that was sent it to me before Christmas with instructions not to open the package until Christmas Eve. I was so surprised to find a DVD. My family was able to watch this meaningful gift together and we were all blessed and touched by the friends who participated and helped put it together. This gift was especially meaningful at the time, because my cancer had taken a turn for the worse and we weren't at all sure what the future would hold.

64. Shop for jewelry with words of encouragement. For example, several silver circles on a chain, with each circle stating one word like "strength", "faith", or "hope". There are many words that convey a positive message. This kind of jewelry is often found in small gift shops, boutiques or street fairs.

65. Purchase jewelry with angels, such as a necklace with an angel charm. A cross for a Christian friend is meaningful. Local Christian stores have a wide variety of inspiring items to purchase in addition to jewelry.

66. If your friend is a Christian, review the products on www. encouragement.com. They offer a variety of Christian products, including crosses, mugs, and picture frames. All their products, no matter how large or small, contain Scripture somewhere on the gift.

67. Design personalized stationary, notepads or gift cards. A fun website for this is www.Designhergals.com. On the site you may design a woman from a wide array of choices of her hair color and style, clothes, accessories, even her body type. It is similar to playing with paper dolls as a child. The idea is to make the woman look somewhat like your friend. The company will print your girl on stationary, notepads, or on an assortment of products. You may also print your friend's name on the stationary. This company donates a percentage

of each sale to an organization supporting advanced

breast cancer. They have sales extremely often which

helps with the cost.

Gifts During Radiation

R adiation treatments often cause fatigue. The tiredness is usually more severe towards the end of the radiation treatments or after the treatment ends. For some people, this fatigue can last several months. Many of the gifts that follow relate to helping the cancer patient when she is tired.

68. Offer to drive the cancer patient to radiation once a week or more often if you are available. Most radiation treatments are set up to be at the same time on Monday through Friday each week.

69. Bring a take-out lunch over and eat with her if she is forced to cancel activities due to fatigue. It's important for her not to feel isolated from her friends.

70. If the weather is nice, talk with a few friends and pack a picnic lunch to share with the patient, meeting as a group at her home. Be sure to include pretty paper plates and cups, silverware, and a blanket or table-cloth. All the ill person has to do is sit back and relax and enjoy her thoughtful friends.

71. Donate babysitting time to a young, overwhelmed mom. This gives her a break from her children and gives her the opportunity to take a nap, workout, or run errands..

72. Offer to drive the family children to lessons, sports practices, or school.

73. Purchase a spa gift card for any treatment offered. A massage or facial might be a real boost to someone who is fatigued.

74. Make up a basket of small presents each wrapped in paper and ribbons; one to be opened after each radia-

tion treatment. This was such a fun surprise for me from a friend! I found the basket at my door when I arrived home from my first radiation treatment. My treatments were every day for 33 days, and I found 33 small gift-wrapped presents in the basket. This was a real labor of love, and could be done by several friends. It was so much fun to look forward to opening a present each day! They were all inexpensive, small but thoughtful gifts.

75. Paula and Cathy planted flowers in my yard. I looked out the front window one day and there they were, digging holes in the dirt. They had all the tools, extra soil, fertilizer, and a watering can in addition to some beautiful flowers. They found the hose and completed the project. What a loving gift!

76. Buy an assortment of new birthday, anniversary or friendship cards for the tired woman to mail to others. Going to the store and choosing cards takes more energy than many patients want to expend. Having

cards available enables them to keep up with their own friends' birthdays and special days.

77. Purchase wrapping paper, ribbon, or assorted gift bags for your ill friend to use for her own presents to others. This avoids any extra shopping trips when she wants to give a gift.

78. Help with Christmas shopping, either online or in stores.

79. Wrap her Christmas presents. Bring the wrapping paper, ribbon, tape and scissors with you and wrap at her home if she wants company. If not, take them back to your home to wrap.

80. Help the stressed woman compose a grocery list. Shop and deliver the groceries to her.

81. Continue to send your friend invitations for parties, showers, or get-togethers. This helps the ill one to feel included, and leaves the choice of attending up to her.

82. Celebrate the final radiation treatment with the patient's friends. Have a simple surprise congratulations party, perhaps sneaking into your friend's home and being

there when she returns from the final treatment. A husband or roommate could help with the surprise. A word of caution: my Bible study group was going to surprise me in my home after the last radiation treatment, but they had the wrong time and I was still at home. I thought someone was breaking into the house when I heard the noise!

83. Gather friends at the doctor's office during the patient's final radiation treatment. Surprise her with a trip to a yogurt or ice cream store.

In Closing

"Keep on loving each other as brothers."

Hebrews 13:1

L earning to receive gifts is a humbling and life altering experience. The receiver is fortunate to get a glimpse into the beautiful side of the human heart. Friends and relatives want to do something to help the patient feel better and to cheer her up. They want to surprise her with a present they have chosen especially for her. The true gift for the ill person is the joy of knowing that God put her on the mind of another, and she is special. There is no better way to navigate a setback than to feel surrounded by thoughtful, empathetic, and caring people who love and support you through your illness.

About the Author

Luke 6:31

"Do to others as you would have them do to you."

I was diagnosed with breast cancer in 1998, and have had metastatic, or advanced cancer, since 2001. I have been through several surgeries, various times of being on chemotherapy drug treatment, and weeks of both breast and later, brain radiation treatments. During those harder times, I had the experience of being on the receiving end of gifts. My friends have meant so much to me with their fun surprises, heart felt notes, and touching phone calls. Prayer has always been one of my favorites, as it reminds me who is really in charge of my disease. Whenever I have had to face a new challenge, I have been blessed with much love and support. I wanted to share some of these ideas with you, in hopes you will access them when your friends or family members face a difficult disease or a surgery of some type.

In addition………………..

Please know that living with a long-term chronic illness such as Rheumatoid Arthritis, Multiple Sclerosis, Parkinson's or metastatic cancer does not mean a person is feeling horrid every day. The afflicted person may be feeling good much of the time, with an occasional flare-up of their disease. From my point of view in dealing with long-term cancer, the stricken person wants to be seen as healthy when they are feeling well. There are enough doctor visits, tests, and drugs to remind them of their own disease, and being seen as healthy is refreshing. The suggestions in this book are gifts to be used during the stressful, more critical days of an illness or surgery.

Acknowledgments

Thank you to my friends in the desert and in Eugene. I love you all and thank you for your support over the years.

To my sister Jinny, who has taken care of me through several surgeries and is always there for me when I need her.

To my husband, Barry, who has supported me through so much. I love you with my whole heart.

To the following people for help with editing: Sheila Smith, Peggy Schluchter, Jinny and Scott Wilcott, and Barry Sterett.

To Jackie Moothart for her constant love, mentoring, and encouragement to finish the book.

For More Information Contact:
Jane Sterett
jsterett62@aol.com
or, 760-321-9064

9 781612 153919